Amazing
Snakes

WRITTEN BY
ALEXANDRA PARSONS

PHOTOGRAPHED BY
JERRY YOUNG

DK

Dorling Kindersley · London

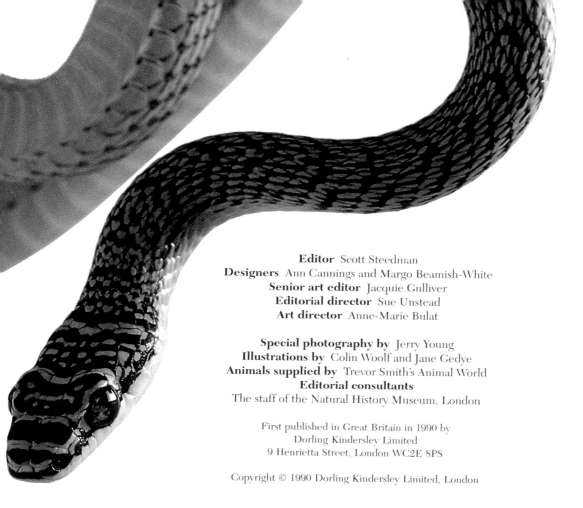

Editor Scott Steedman
Designers Ann Cannings and Margo Beamish-White
Senior art editor Jacquie Gulliver
Editorial director Sue Unstead
Art director Anne-Marie Bulat

Special photography by Jerry Young
Illustrations by Colin Woolf and Jane Gedye
Animals supplied by Trevor Smith's Animal World
Editorial consultants
The staff of the Natural History Museum, London

First published in Great Britain in 1990 by
Dorling Kindersley Limited
9 Henrietta Street, London WC2E 8PS

British Library Cataloguing in Publication Data
Parsons, Alexandra
Amazing snakes
1. Snakes
I. Title   II. Series
597.96

ISBN 0-86318-432-4

Colour reproduction by Colourscan, Singapore
Typeset by Windsorgraphics, Ringwood, Hampshire
Printed in Italy by A. Mondadori Editore, Verona

Contents

What is a snake?

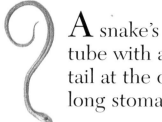

A snake's body is like a long tube with a head at one end, a tail at the other end, and a great long stomach in between.

Poison or the squeeze?
Some snakes kill their prey with poison, which they inject with their fangs. Others wrap themselves around their victims and squeeze them to death.

Snakes never wink or blink because they don't have eyelids.

Taste that smell!
A snake can smell out other animals by "tasting" the air with its forked tongue. It passes any pongs it finds back to a special sense organ in its mouth.

"smelling organ"

Fresh meat
Many snakes eat their meals while the meal is still alive!

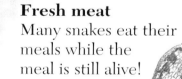

There are many different kinds of kingsnake, and each kind has a different pattern of colourful rings.

Snake-eating snake
This Californian kingsnake is harmless to humans. It eats small animals, birds, and snakes – even poisonous ones like rattlesnakes.

The big swallow

Snakes can't chew their food before they eat it, so they have to swallow their victims whole. Their jaw bones are held together by a sort of elastic band, so they can open their mouths up very wide.

Snake bones

Snakes have very long backbones and so many ribs you'd get muddled trying to count them all.

Sshh!

Snakes don't have ears like we do. They "feel" sounds by picking up vibrations in the ground.

Snakes have very complicated joints in their backbones, which allow them to bend in almost any direction.

The sunbeam snake

This snake has beautiful skin that shimmers like a rainbow in the sunlight. But it spends most of its life hidden away in a dark burrow in the ground.

The sunbeam snake lives in the watery rice fields of China and Indonesia.

Snake skin
A snake's skin is made up of hundreds of tiny scales which overlap like tiles on a roof.

Friendly fellows
There are 2,700 different kinds of snake in the world, divided into 30 family groups. Most of them are harmless to humans.

Long, cool, and dry
Snakes aren't wet and slimy. Their skin is actually dry and cool. It only looks wet because it shines in the light.

Shedding skin

All that slithering wears out a snake's skin. So several times a year the snake crawls out of its old skin, revealing a shiny new layer that's grown underneath.

Shedding starts at the snake's head.

A snake's shadow

A snake may shed its skin in one complete piece. When it does this, it leaves behind an eerie, see-through, inside-out image of its body.

A winter snooze

In places where it gets cold in the winter, snakes "sleep" through the coldest months. This is called hibernating. Some snakes hibernate in dens or caves, while others curl up inside hollow trees.

11

The big squeeze

The reticulated python is one of the biggest, longest, and strongest snakes in the whole world. It's not poisonous but it can squeeze the life out of a small deer.

Catch me if you can

Most of the stories about pythons eating people are fairy tales. Very few snakes are big enough to swallow a human, and really big snakes are so fat and slow they'd be very lucky to catch one!

King size

Ask a grown-up to take ten giant steps, and mark where he or she starts and finishes. That should be about 10 m, the length of the longest python. It was found in the jungles of Thailand in Asia.

A very solid snake

The heaviest snake in the world is the anaconda. A really big anaconda can have a body as thick as a barrel and weigh 180 kg – that's as much as three grown men.

A python is patterned to match the leaves on the forest floor.

Squeeze me

A python can squeeze the life out of a goat or a wild pig in less than a minute.

Snake hips

Pythons are descended from prehistoric lizards that lived at the same time as the dinosaurs. They still have tiny, useless pegs where their hips and legs used to be.

Gulp!

Would you believe that a python can swallow a whole goat? Well, it can. Snakes don't chew or swallow the way we do. They open their jaws wide around the prey and simply "climb" forward until it disappears down their throat.

The egg-eater

There is a group of snakes that eats nothing but birds' eggs. They swallow the egg whole, squash it, enjoy the insides, and spit out the shell.

Stretchy skin

The egg-eater is a slim snake with very stretchy skin that won't burst if it swallows an enormous egg.

Night worker

This egg-eating snake comes from Africa. It sleeps during the day and searches for eggs at night.

special spikes *backbone*

Toothless

An egg-eating snake doesn't have many teeth, so it won't break the egg by accident while swallowing it.

Sawbones

The egg-eater has a row of special sharp spikes that stick down from the back of its throat. Once it has swallowed an egg, the snake bends its head down, pushing the egg up against these spikes. This cuts a slit in the eggshell so the insides come gushing out.

The egg-eating snake can swallow a bird's egg twice the size of its head.

Squish squash
Getting rid of the eggshell is quite hard work. The snake tightens its muscles to crush the shell and then spits it out in a nice neat bundle. The whole egg-eating process takes about 15 minutes.

before   *after*

Lazybones
Like some people, snakes move only if they are hot, hungry, or frightened. Otherwise they are quite happy to lie about all day doing nothing.

The deadly cobra

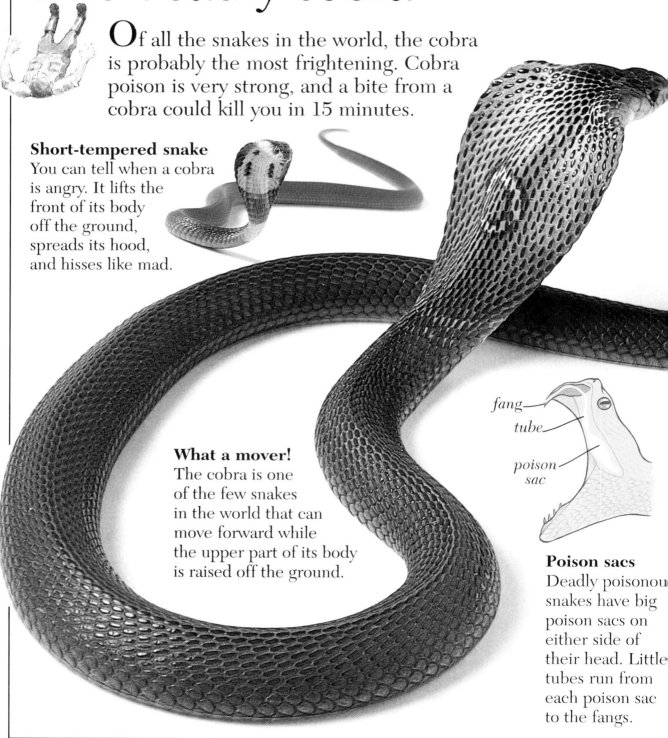

Of all the snakes in the world, the cobra is probably the most frightening. Cobra poison is very strong, and a bite from a cobra could kill you in 15 minutes.

Short-tempered snake

You can tell when a cobra is angry. It lifts the front of its body off the ground, spreads its hood, and hisses like mad.

What a mover!

The cobra is one of the few snakes in the world that can move forward while the upper part of its body is raised off the ground.

fang
tube
poison sac

Poison sacs

Deadly poisonou snakes have big poison sacs on either side of their head. Little tubes run from each poison sac to the fangs.

A scary story

The Greeks have a legend about a terrible monster called Medusa who had snakes instead of hair. She was so ugly that anyone who looked at her was turned to stone. A brave and clever hero called Perseus, using his shiny shield as a mirror, managed to lop off Medusa's head without looking at her hideous face.

A sad story

Long ago, there was a beautiful queen of Egypt called Cleopatra who was very sad because the man she loved had died. She killed herself by letting one of the royal cobras bite her.

Dangerous babies

Cobras can bite and kill as soon as they hatch from their eggs. Just one tablespoon of their dried poison could kill 165 people, or over 160,000 mice.

How charming!

Snake charmers can make snakes dance to their music. At least that's what it looks like. In fact, the snake can't even hear the music and is just copying the swaying movements of the charmer and the flute.

Don't spit!

Some cobras, called spitting cobras, have a very nasty habit. When they feel threatened, they squirt jets of poison into their attacker's eyes.

The rattlesnake

This snake is one of the fastest killers in the animal world. It glides forward silently, strikes suddenly, and its poison is deadly.

Its scaly, patterned skin makes the rattlesnake hard to see when it's coiled up under a pile of leaves.

Baby snakes

Most snakes lay eggs. But rattlesnakes give birth to live babies. The mother leaves the baby snakes to look after them-selves as soon as they are born.

Rattle, rattle

The rattlesnake gets its name from the rattling sound its tail makes. The rattly bits are little hollow rings that fit inside one another. When the snake wants to frighten its enemies, it shakes its rattle very fast.

Each time a rattlesnake sheds its skin, a new ring is added to the tail. The rings are made of the same stuff as your toenails.

Pyjama party

Rattlesnakes gather in groups to sleep through the winter. Sometimes up to 1,000 of them will coil up together.

What a job!

Snake poison, also called venom, is an important ingredient in some medicines. To collect the venom, people who have been specially trained for the job "milk" the snakes – very, very carefully!

Look out!

Rattlesnakes are the most dangerous snakes in America. They only bite people if they're trodden on by mistake, so if you're walking around in the American desert, watch where you put your feet!

The milk snake

This is one of the most colourful snakes of all. It is not poisonous. It eats mice and birds, which it kills by squeezing.

The milk snake lives and hunts under logs and rotting leaves.

coral snake

Confusing colours
The milk snake looks very like the deadly coral snake, which has stripes of the same colour but in a different order. Here is a little rhyme to help you tell which is which:

Red to yellow, kill a fellow,
Red to black, venom lack.

Blending in
Some snakes are very well "camouflaged". This means that their patterns blend in with the background so that enemies find it hard to see them.

Unlucky for some
Milk snakes lay about 13 eggs – in heaps of animal manure.

egg tooth

Let me out!
Baby snakes get out of their eggs all by themselves. They have a special little "egg tooth" to saw through the shell.

Does it drink milk?
No, it doesn't. People used to think that the milk snake would sneak into cowsheds to suck milk from cows. It does sneak into cowsheds, but it's looking for mice, not milk.

Keep reading
A snake expert is called a herpetologist (*her-puh-tol-uh-jist*). That's what you will be when you finish reading this book.

The world's smallest snake
This honour goes to the rare thread snake of the West Indies. If you could take the lead out of a pencil, the tiny thread snake could slither through the hole.

A snake that flies?

In the hot and steamy jungles of Asia lives the amazing flying snake. This beautiful animal can leap into the air and glide from tree to tree.

The flying snake takes off by uncoiling quickly, like a spring.

Yippee, bats for tea!
A flying snake enjoys a diet of lizards, birds, frogs, and bats, which it kills with poison and then swallows head first.

ribs

Flat out
Flying snakes glide through the air by pushing out their ribs and holding in their bellies until they're flat like a ribbon.

Skydiving
Flying snakes don't really fly. They glide through the air in a giant S-shape.

The rough scales on the snake's belly help it to climb trees.

When danger strikes
Flying snakes don't take off too often – only when they're in danger of attack from hawks or eagles soaring overhead.

Looping the loop
The flying snake can only "fly" downward or across, not up. But it can steer in the air by twisting its body this way and that.

The tree boa

These handsome snakes live in the jungles of South America. They kill by squeezing and have a very clever way of hunting – by "feeling" the heat from their victims' bodies.

Where's my lunch?
The hungry tree boa hangs from branches and swings its head from side to side. When it feels exactly the same amount of heat on both sides, it knows that a meal is right in front of it.

Fearsome fangs
The tree boa's closed mouth hides its very long, sharp front teeth for catching fast-moving birds and bats.

Monkey business
The tree boa uses its strong tail to grab hold of branches, almost like a monkey does. It can hold more than half of its body suspended in mid air.

Flying meal
All kinds of small creatures can end up on a boa's dinner menu, from bats to rats. The emerald tree boa even snatches birds on the wing.

Bath night
Tree boas leave their trees only to go for a swim in a jungle river or for a quick slither in a swamp.

heat spots

Like many snakes that live in trees, Cook's tree boa is lightly coloured on its belly and dark on top. From above it blends in with the forest floor, and from below with the sky.

Hunting for warmth
The boa can tell if there is a nice meal hiding nearby, even in total darkness. It has little holes on its lips that can "feel" an animal's body heat.

Hanging loose
A tree boa doesn't coil itself around its branch. Instead, it just flops over the branch in loops, ready to straighten out and hurl itself at a victim.

Poached or fried?
If you ever find yourself dining out with some Indians in the Amazon jungle, don't be surprised if they serve you up a slice or two of tree boa.

The vine snake

This long, thin snake lies very still in its tree, waiting for something tasty to pass by. Wrapped around a branch, it looks like a harmless piece of jungle vine.

Watching and waiting

The vine snake has very good eyesight. Both its eyes face forward, like ours do, so the snake can judge distances as it goes in for the kill. Its head is long and pointed, rather like Concorde's nose.

A vine snake may grow longer than your leg, but it will never get much fatter than your finger.

Thirsty?

Tree snakes drink dew and rainwater from leaves. Snakes that live on the ground get their drinking water from grass, moss, and puddles of rain.

Quick as a wink

The vine snake may stay still for hours and hours, but when it finally moves, it's as fast as lightning. It can snatch a bird or lizard in a third of a second. That's about the time it takes to blink.

Killer juices

The digestive juices of most snakes are so strong they can turn bones into mush.

Most trees are green, and so are most tree snakes.

Back teeth

The vine snake has fangs at the back of its mouth so it can give its lunch a jab of poison on the way down. More deadly snakes like cobras have fangs at the very fronts of their mouths.

poison sac

fangs

How snakes move

Moving along without legs or arms could be a little difficult, but snakes have found a way. In fact, they have found four main ways.

Sidewinding
This "sidestepping" movement is ideal for soft sand, which is hard to grip. From an S-shaped position on the ground, the snake flicks its head a metre or two to one side. Then it pulls the rest of its body up to its head to form another S-shape – ready to start again.

Cool belly
When moving like this, the snake's belly hardly touches the hot sand. This is one reason why some desert snakes get about by sidewinding. This sidewinder is found in the scorching deserts of the American West.

Not so fast
Don't worry – you could easily outrun a snake. Snakes don't move very fast and they get tired quickly. The fastest ones can slither along at about the same speed as a person walking, but they cannot keep up the pace for more than a few minutes.

Concertina
This movement is good for tight spots. The snake bunches up its body in loops and then straightens out, pushing its head forward. Then it pulls its tail up to join the rest of the body.

Wriggling
To wriggle, the snake pushes against rocks or other hard objects, first on one side and then on the other. Its body seems to move forward in waves.

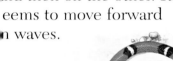

When a snake is creeping, its body is almost straight. All you can see are ripples running down its back.

Creeping
Fat snakes, like pythons, can creep along. They slide their skin to and fro, using the scales on their bellies to grip.

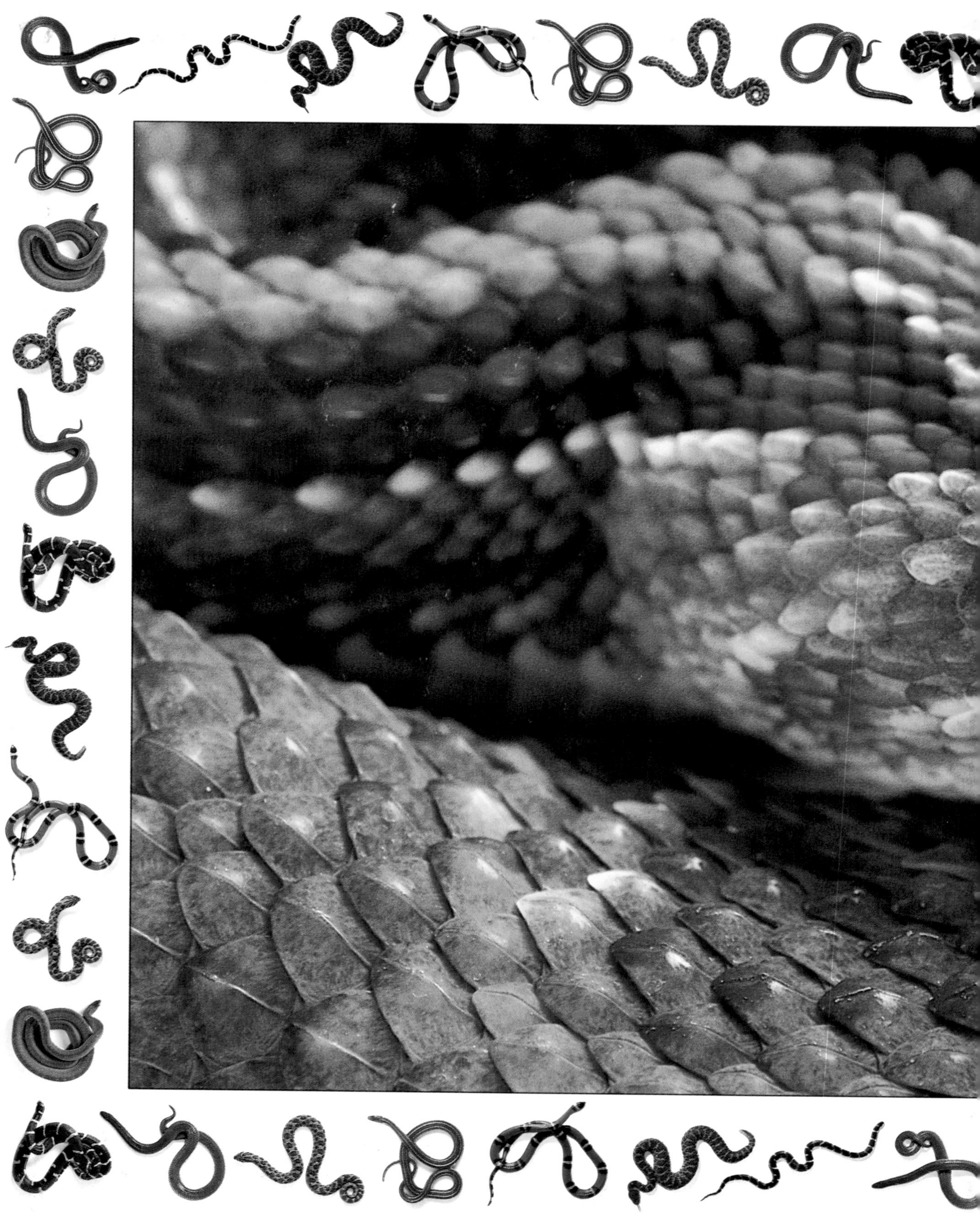